Jonas Brothers

ABDO
Publishing Company

A Big Buddy Book
by **Sarah Tieck**

VISIT US AT

www.abdopublishing.com

Published by ABDO Publishing Company, 8000 West 78th Street, Edina, Minnesota 55439.

Printed in the United States.

Coordinating Series Editor: Rochelle Baltzer
Contributing Editor: Marcia Zappa
Graphic Design: Maria Hosley
Cover Photograph: *AP Photo*: Sipa via AP Images
Interior Photographs/Illustrations: *AP Photo*: Evan Agostini (pp. 25, 27), Peter Kramer (p. 15), Matt Sayles (p. 29),
    Sipa via AP Images (p. 24), Mark J. Terrill (p. 14); *Getty Images*: Ida Mae Astute/ABC via Getty Images (p. 21),
    E. Charbonneau/WireImage for Disney Pictures (p. 18), David Hogan (pp. 11, 13, 23), Sandy Huffaker (p. 5),
    Kevin Parry (p. 7), Kevin Winter (p. 17); *iStockPhoto*: Solidago (p. 8), Aimin Tang (p. 8); *Photos.com* (p. 8);
    Wikipedia.com (p. 12).

Library of Congress Cataloging-in-Publication Data

Tieck, Sarah, 1976-
   Jonas Brothers / Sarah Tieck.
      p. cm. -- (Big buddy biographies)
   ISBN 978-1-60453-549-5
   1. Jonas Brothers (Musical group)--Juvenile literature. 2. Rock musicians--United States--Biography--Juvenile
literature. I. Title.

   ML3930.J62T54 2009
   782.42164092'2--dc22
   [B]
                              2008033923

Contents

Singing Stars

Kevin, Joe, and Nick Jonas are **musicians**. The brothers sing, play instruments, and write songs. They are members of a band called Jonas Brothers.

The boys act on television, too. They appeared in Disney's *Camp Rock*.

Nick (*left*) and Joe (*middle*) take turns as lead singer of Jonas Brothers. Kevin (*right*) sings backup. And, all three play instruments.

Family Ties

Kevin, Joe, and Nick are brothers. Paul Kevin "Kevin" Jonas II was born on November 5, 1987. Joseph Adam "Joe" Jonas was born August 15, 1989. And, Nicholas Jerry "Nick" Jonas was born September 16, 1992.

Their parents are Kevin Sr. and Denise Jonas. They have a younger brother named Frankie. His **nickname** is "Bonus Jonas."

Did you know...

Kevin is named for his father. Sometimes he is called "K2."

Denise was a special education teacher. Now, she and Kevin Sr. travel with their sons for concert tours.

Frankie travels with his parents and brothers. He and Nick share a bunk bed.

Arizona

New Jersey

UNITED STATES

PACIFIC OCEAN

ATLANTIC OCEAN

Texas

N
W E
S

The Jonas brothers each have a different birthplace. Kevin was born in Teaneck, New Jersey. Joe was born in Casa Grande, Arizona. And Nick was born in Dallas, Texas.

Over the years, the family traveled and moved many times. Then, Kevin Sr. became a church pastor in Wyckoff, New Jersey. The Jonases settled there.

Growing Up

The Jonas brothers come from a musical family. They sang with their parents in church choirs. Their parents wrote Christian songs and sometimes helped record albums.

When the boys were growing up, the family traveled with Christian bands. This was part of Kevin Sr.'s work with Christ for the Nations Music.

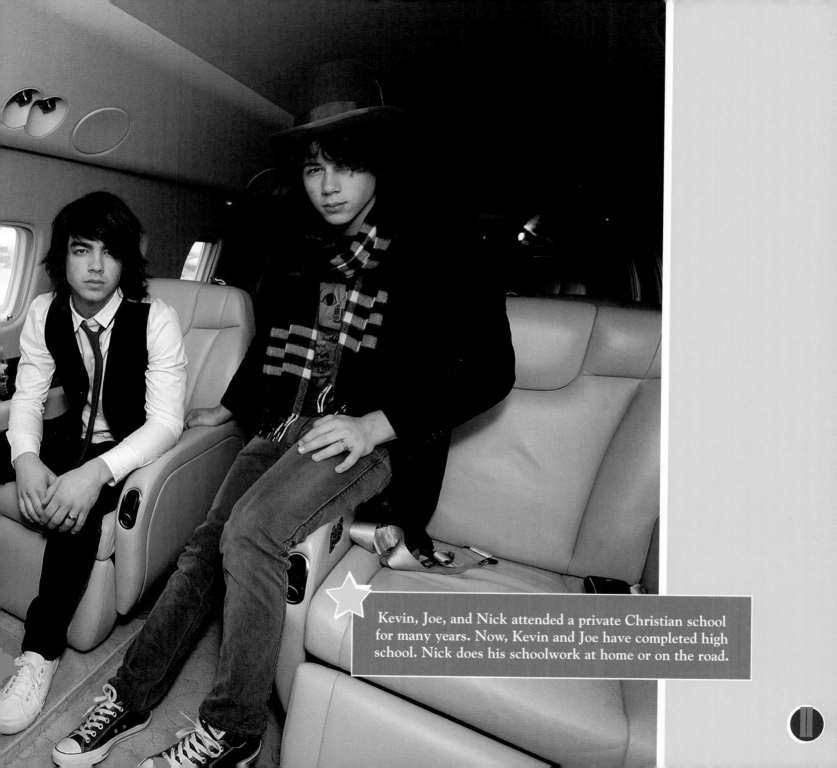

Kevin, Joe, and Nick attended a private Christian school for many years. Now, Kevin and Joe have completed high school. Nick does his schoolwork at home or on the road.

Working Alone

Nick was the first Jonas to enter the music business. He was discovered at age six while singing during a haircut! By eight, he had debuted in a Broadway show.

Nick wanted to sing professionally. In 2002, he and his dad wrote a song. "Joy to the World (A Christmas Prayer)" helped more people notice Nick's talent. And in 2004, he released an album called *Nicholas Jonas*.

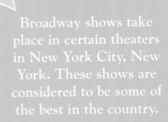

Broadway shows take place in certain theaters in New York City, New York. These shows are considered to be some of the best in the country.

Nick has always wanted to be a singer. At just three years old, he sang into pretend microphones!

13

At first, Joe and Kevin weren't interested in working as **musicians**. Instead, they appeared in television **commercials**. Soon, they decided to work on their musical talent.

Joe had never enjoyed **opera**. But in 2002, he had an opportunity to show his talent. Joe sang in the opera *La Bohéme* on Broadway.

When Kevin was 12, he taught himself to play **guitar**. He loved it and decided to join a band.

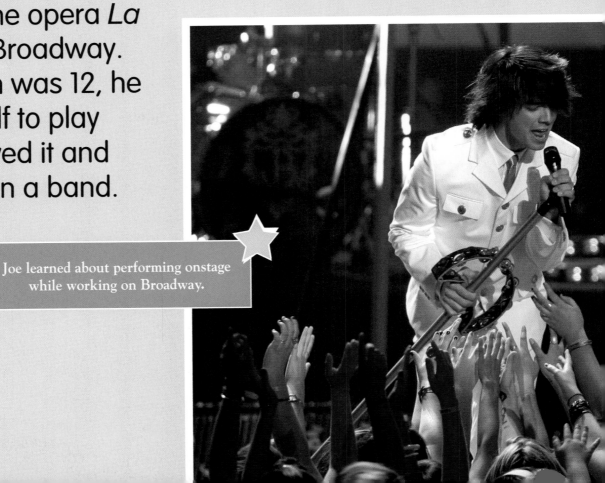

Joe learned about performing onstage while working on Broadway.

Kevin first learned to play guitar from reading a book!

Becoming a Band

Sometimes, Kevin and Joe helped Nick practice his music. Their voices sounded good together. So in 2005, they formed a pop rock band called Jonas Brothers. Their first album, *It's About Time*, was **released** in 2006.

The first Jonas Brothers song released was "Mandy." This song was popular with fans.

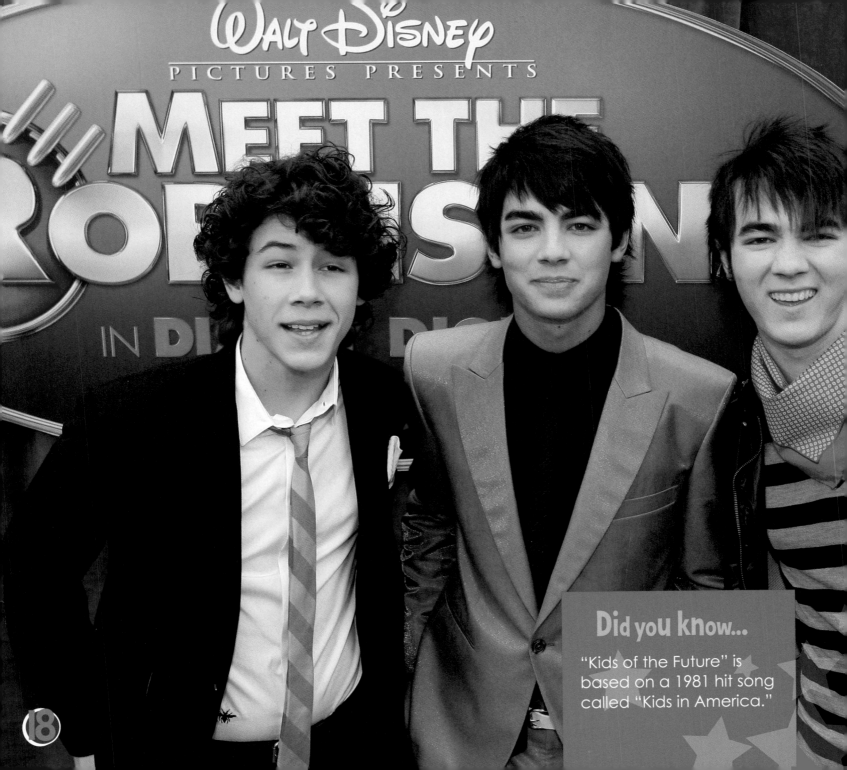

Did you know...

"Kids of the Future" is based on a 1981 hit song called "Kids in America."

Making It Big

The first Jonas Brothers album did not sell well. But, the brothers continued performing and writing music. They didn't want to give up their dream.

They toured with Kelly Clarkson, the Backstreet Boys, and the Cheetah Girls. They gained many fans. Soon, their songs played regularly on the Disney Channel.

In 2007, Kevin, Joe, and Nick **released** their second album, *Jonas Brothers*. This album had the fifth-highest sales in the United States for almost three weeks! The brothers became very popular. In 2008, they appeared on *The Oprah Winfrey Show* and *Dancing with the Stars*. Also, *People* magazine featured them in stories.

In 2007, Jonas Brothers and Miley Cyrus sang in a New Year's Eve television show.

Lights! Camera! Action!

Soon, the Jonas brothers began to star in television shows. In May 2008, Disney Channel made a show about their lives. It is called *Jonas Brothers: Living the Dream*. The show features the brothers backstage and on the road.

Did you know...

The Jonas Brothers tour bus is like a scrapbook. Fans painted their names on its side. Some even wrote messages for Kevin, Joe, and Nick.

Before each concert, Kevin, Joe, and Nick spend 40 minutes getting ready. They get dressed, warm up their voices, and relax.

23

In June 2008, Kevin, Joe, and Nick appeared in Disney Channel's *Camp Rock*. Joe had a starring **role**! He played Shane Gray, the lead singer of a band. Nick and Kevin played Shane's bandmates.

Camp Rock is one of the Disney Channel's most successful movies. Almost 9 million people watched its **debut**!

In *Camp Rock*, Nick, Joe, and Kevin play rock stars in a band called Connect 3.

Camp Rock

Camp Rock is a story about being yourself and following your dreams. The story takes place at a music camp called Camp Rock.

In the movie, Mitchie Torres dreams of being a singer. She meets rock star Shane Gray at the camp. Mitchie helps him remember his love for music.

The cast of *Camp Rock* has appeared in magazines and on television. Fans can purchase clothes, toys, books, albums, and DVDs.

Jonas Brothers fans were
excited to see them in a movie.

Buzz

Kevin, Joe, and Nick own a home together in Vaquero, Texas. They also spend time in Los Angeles, California.

In 2008, they **released** their third album, *A Little Bit Longer*. They performed at many sold-out concerts. They also began work on more Disney Channel shows and movies, including *Camp Rock 2*.

Kevin, Joe, and Nick continue to grow more successful. Fans expect great things from Jonas Brothers!

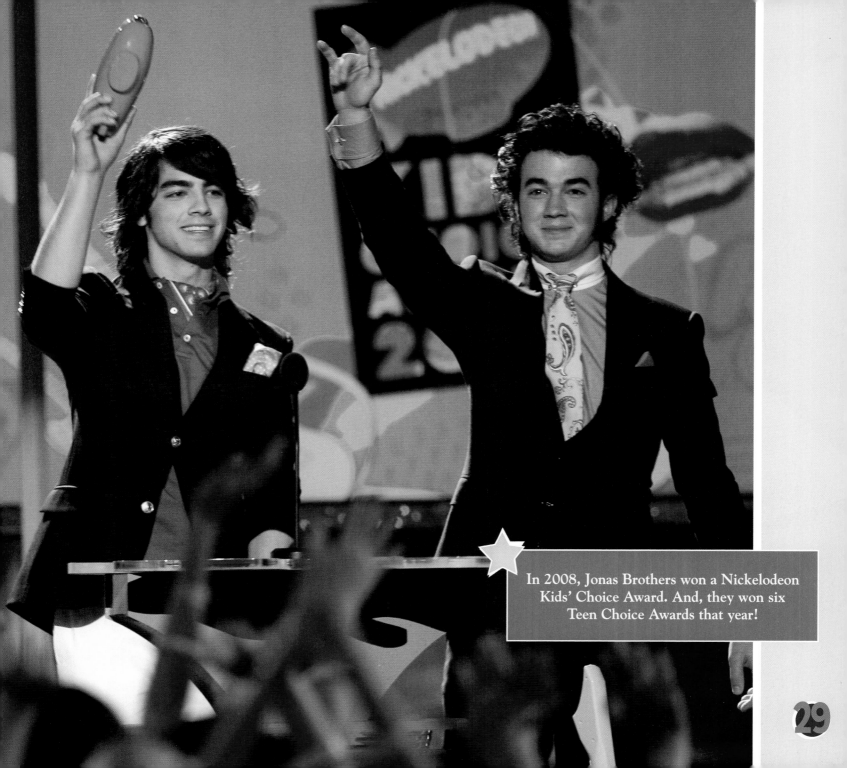

In 2008, Jonas Brothers won a Nickelodeon Kids' Choice Award. And, they won six Teen Choice Awards that year!

Snapshot

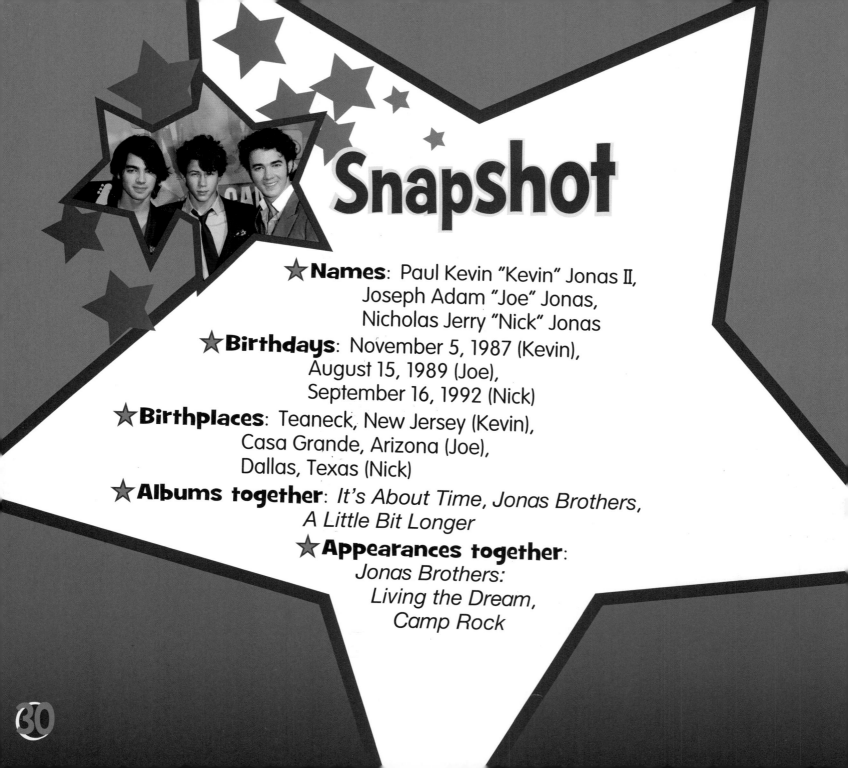

⭐ **Names**: Paul Kevin "Kevin" Jonas II,
Joseph Adam "Joe" Jonas,
Nicholas Jerry "Nick" Jonas

⭐ **Birthdays**: November 5, 1987 (Kevin),
August 15, 1989 (Joe),
September 16, 1992 (Nick)

⭐ **Birthplaces**: Teaneck, New Jersey (Kevin),
Casa Grande, Arizona (Joe),
Dallas, Texas (Nick)

⭐ **Albums together**: *It's About Time, Jonas Brothers,
A Little Bit Longer*

⭐ **Appearances together**:
*Jonas Brothers:
Living the Dream,
Camp Rock*

Important Words

commercial (kuh-MUHR-shuhl) a short message on television or radio that helps sell a product.

debut (DAY-byoo) to make a first appearance.

guitar (guh-TAHR) a stringed musical instrument played by strumming.

musician someone who writes, sings, or plays music.

nickname a name that replaces a person's real name.

opera a play that is mostly sung, with costumes, scenery, acting, and music.

professional (pruh-FEHSH-nuhl) working for money rather than for pleasure.

release to make available to the public.

role a part an actor plays in a show.

Web Sites

To learn more about Jonas Brothers, visit ABDO Publishing Company online. Web sites about Jonas Brothers are featured on our Book Links page. These links are routinely monitored and updated to provide the most current information available.

www.abdopublishing.com

Index